PASTRIES MADE SIMPLE

RECIPES

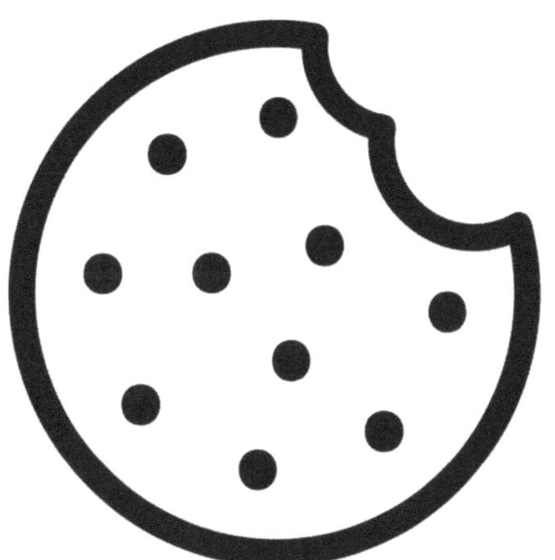

Belong to

....

....

....

The Pastries Made Simple is one of the eight cookbooks published as part of a larger collection designed to help you write your own recipes in one place and have them at hand when you cook your favorite meals.

This **Special Collection** also includes:

- **SOUPS**
- **SALADS**
- **APPETIZERS**
- **DIET RECIPES**
- **OVEN RECIPES**
- **VEGAN RECIPES**
- **CAKES AND PIES**

Table of Contents

Recipe   **Page**

Table of Contents

Recipe	Page

Table of Contents

Recipe

Page

Table of Contents

Recipe	Page

Table of Contents

Recipe   Page

Recipe:_______________________________

Prep time:________   Cook time:________   Servings:________

Ingredients

Directions

Notes

Recipe:____

Prep time:________   Cook time:________   Servings:________

Ingredients

Directions

Notes

Recipe:____

Prep time:________   Cook time:________   Servings:________

Ingredients   ## Directions

Notes

Recipe:____

Prep time:________   Cook time:________   Servings:________

Ingredients

Directions

Notes

Recipe:____

Prep time:_______   Cook time:_______   Servings:_______

Ingredients

Directions

Notes

Recipe:_______________________________________

Prep time:_______ Cook time:_______ Servings:_______

Ingredients

Directions

Notes

Recipe:_______________________________

Prep time:______   Cook time:______   Servings:______

Ingredients

Directions

Notes

Recipe:____

Prep time:________   Cook time:________   Servings:________

Ingredients

Directions

Notes

Recipe:_______________________________________

Prep time:________   Cook time:________   Servings:________

Ingredients

Directions

Notes

Recipe:

Prep time: ______ **Cook time:** ______ **Servings:** ______

Ingredients

Directions

Notes

Recipe:____

Prep time:______   Cook time:______   Servings:______

Ingredients

Directions

Notes

Recipe:____

Prep time:_______   Cook time:_______   Servings:_______

Ingredients

Directions

Notes

Recipe:____

Prep time:________ Cook time:________ Servings:________

Ingredients

Directions

Notes

Recipe:____

Prep time:_______   Cook time:_______   Servings:_______

Ingredients

Directions

Notes

Recipe:____

Prep time:_________   Cook time:_________   Servings:_________

Ingredients

Directions

Notes

Recipe:_______________________________________

Prep time:_______ **Cook time:**_______ **Servings:**_______

Ingredients	Directions

Notes

Recipe:_______________________________________

Prep time:_______   Cook time:_______   Servings:_______

Ingredients

Directions

Notes

Recipe:____

Prep time:_______   Cook time:_______   Servings:_______

Ingredients

Directions

Notes

Recipe:____

Prep time:________   Cook time:________   Servings:________

Ingredients

....

....

....

....

....

....

....

....

....

....

....

....

....

Directions

....

....

....

....

....

....

....

....

....

....

....

....

....

Notes

....

....

....

Recipe:____

Prep time:_______   Cook time:_______   Servings:_______

| Ingredients | Directions |

Notes

Recipe:_______________________________________

Prep time:_______   Cook time:_______   Servings:_______

Ingredients

Directions

Notes

Recipe:____

Prep time:________   Cook time:________   Servings:________

Ingredients	Directions

Notes

Recipe:_______________________________________

Prep time:________   Cook time:________   Servings:________

Ingredients

Directions

Notes

Recipe:____

Prep time:_______ **Cook time:**_______ **Servings:**_______

Ingredients	Directions

Notes

Recipe:

Prep time: Cook time: Servings:

Ingredients

Directions

Notes

Recipe:____

Prep time:_______   Cook time:_______   Servings:_______

Ingredients	Directions

Notes

Recipe:____

Prep time:________   Cook time:________   Servings:________

Ingredients

Directions

Notes

Recipe:_______________________________________

Prep time:_______   Cook time:_______   Servings:_______

Ingredients

Directions

Notes

Recipe:_______________________________________

Prep time:_______   Cook time:_______   Servings:_______

Ingredients

Directions

Notes

Recipe:_______________________

Prep time:______ **Cook time:**______ **Servings:**______

Ingredients	Directions

Notes

Recipe:

Prep time: _______ **Cook time:** _______ **Servings:** _______

Ingredients

Directions

Notes

Recipe:____

Prep time:_______   Cook time:________   Servings:_______

Ingredients	Directions

Notes

Recipe:____

Prep time:________   Cook time:________   Servings:________

Ingredients

Directions

Notes

Recipe:_______________________________________

Prep time:_______   Cook time:_______   Servings:_______

Ingredients	Directions

Notes

Recipe:______________________________________

Prep time:________   Cook time:________   Servings:________

Ingredients

Directions

Notes

Recipe:____

Prep time:_______ Cook time:________ Servings:_______

Ingredients

Directions

Notes

Recipe:_______________________________________

Prep time:_______   Cook time:_______   Servings:_______

Ingredients

Directions

Notes

Recipe:_______________________

Prep time:______ **Cook time:**______ **Servings:**______

Ingredients

Directions

Notes

Recipe:________________________________

Prep time:_______ Cook time:_______ Servings:_______

Ingredients	Directions

Notes

Recipe:____

Prep time:_______   Cook time:_______   Servings:_______

Ingredients

Directions

Notes

Recipe:________________________________

Prep time:______ Cook time:______ Servings:______

Ingredients

Directions

Notes

Recipe:_______________________________________

Prep time:________ Cook time:________ Servings:________

Ingredients

Directions

Notes

Recipe:_______________________________________

Prep time:________   Cook time:________   Servings:________

Ingredients

Directions

Notes

Recipe:

Prep time: ______ Cook time: ______ Servings: ______

Ingredients

Directions

Notes

Recipe:_______________________________________

Prep time:________   Cook time:________   Servings:________

Ingredients

Directions

Notes

Recipe:_______________________________________

Prep time:________   Cook time:________   Servings:________

Ingredients

Directions

Notes

Recipe:____

Prep time:_______   Cook time:_______   Servings:_______

Ingredients

Directions

Notes

Recipe:_______________________________________

Prep time:________   Cook time:________   Servings:________

Ingredients

Directions

Notes

Recipe:____

Prep time:________   Cook time:________   Servings:________

Ingredients

Directions

Notes

Recipe:____

Prep time:_______   Cook time:_______   Servings:_______

Ingredients

Directions

Notes

Recipe:_______________________________________

Prep time:________   Cook time:________   Servings:________

Ingredients

Directions

Notes

Recipe:____

Prep time:_______   Cook time:_______   Servings:_______

| Ingredients | Directions |

Notes

Recipe:______________________________________

Prep time:________   Cook time:________   Servings:________

Ingredients

Directions

Notes

Recipe:____

Prep time:_______   Cook time:_______   Servings:_______

Ingredients	Directions

Notes

Recipe:_______________________________________

Prep time:_______   Cook time:_______   Servings:_______

Ingredients

Directions

Notes

Recipe:_______________________________________

Prep time:________   Cook time:________   Servings:________

Ingredients

Directions

Notes

Recipe:

Prep time: _______ **Cook time:** _______ **Servings:** _______

Ingredients

Directions

Notes

Recipe:__________

Prep time:______ Cook time:______ Servings:______

Ingredients

Directions

Notes

Recipe:_______________________________________

Prep time:________   Cook time:________   Servings:________

Ingredients

Directions

....

Notes

Recipe:______________________________

Prep time:______ **Cook time:**______ **Servings:**______

| Ingredients | Directions |

Notes

Recipe:_______________________________________

Prep time:_______   Cook time:_______   Servings:_______

Ingredients

Directions

Notes

Recipe:____

Prep time:_______   Cook time:_______   Servings:_______

Ingredients

Directions

Notes

Recipe:_______________________________

Prep time:______   **Cook time:**______   **Servings:**______

Ingredients	Directions

Notes

Recipe:____

Prep time:________   Cook time:________   Servings:________

Ingredients

Directions

Notes

Recipe:

Prep time:_______ Cook time:_______ Servings:_______

Ingredients

Directions

Notes

Recipe:____

Prep time:______   **Cook time:**______   **Servings:**______

Ingredients	Directions

Notes

Recipe:_______________________________________

Prep time:________   Cook time:________   Servings:________

Ingredients

Directions

Notes

Recipe:___________________________________

Prep time:_______ **Cook time:**_______ **Servings:**_______

Ingredients	Directions

Notes

Recipe:_______________________________________

Prep time:________   Cook time:________   Servings:________

Ingredients

Directions

Notes

Recipe:____

Prep time:________   Cook time:________   Servings:________

Ingredients

Directions

Notes

Prep time:______ Cook time:______ Servings:______

Ingredients

Directions

Notes

Recipe:________________________________

Prep time:______ **Cook time:**______ **Servings:**______

Ingredients	Directions

Notes

Recipe:____

Prep time:________   Cook time:________   Servings:________

Ingredients

Directions

Notes

Recipe:____

Prep time:________   Cook time:________   Servings:________

Ingredients

Directions

Notes

Recipe:_______________________________

Prep time:_______   **Cook time:**_______   **Servings:**_______

Ingredients

Directions

Notes

Recipe:____

Prep time:________   Cook time:________   Servings:________

Ingredients

Directions

Notes

Recipe:_______________________________________

Prep time:________ Cook time:________ Servings:________

Ingredients

Directions

Notes

Recipe:_______________________________________

Prep time:_______   Cook time:_______   Servings:_______

Ingredients

Directions

Notes

Recipe:____

Prep time:________ Cook time:________ Servings:________

Ingredients

Directions

Notes

Recipe:____

Prep time:________   Cook time:________   Servings:________

Ingredients	Directions

Notes

Recipe:____

Prep time:________   Cook time:________   Servings:________

Ingredients

Directions

Notes

Recipe:____

Prep time:_______   Cook time:_______   Servings:_______

Ingredients

Directions

Notes

Recipe:_______________________________________

Prep time:________   Cook time:________   Servings:________

Ingredients

Directions

Notes

Recipe:

Prep time: _______ **Cook time:** _______ **Servings:** _______

Ingredients

Directions

Notes

Recipe:

Prep time: _______ **Cook time:** _______ **Servings:** _______

Ingredients

Directions

Notes

Recipe:

Prep time:______ **Cook time:**______ **Servings:**______

Ingredients

Directions

Notes

Recipe:_______________________________

Prep time:______   **Cook time:**______   **Servings:**______

Ingredients

Directions

Notes

Recipe:____

Prep time:________   Cook time:________   Servings:________

Ingredients	Directions

Notes

Recipe:_______________________________________

Prep time:________   Cook time:________   Servings:________

Ingredients

Directions

Notes

Recipe:____

Prep time:_______ Cook time:_______ Servings:_______

Ingredients

Directions

Notes

Recipe:_______________________________________

Prep time:________   Cook time:________   Servings:________

Ingredients

Directions

Notes

Recipe:________________________________

Prep time:________ **Cook time:**________ **Servings:**________

Ingredients	Directions

Notes

Recipe:_______________________________________

Prep time:_______ **Cook time:**_______ **Servings:**_______

Ingredients | Directions

Notes

Recipe:_______________________________________

Prep time:________   Cook time:________   Servings:________

Ingredients

Directions

Notes

Recipe:____

Prep time:________   Cook time:________   Servings:________

Ingredients

Directions

Notes

Recipe:_____________________________________

Prep time:________   Cook time:________   Servings:________

Ingredients

Directions

Notes

Recipe:

Prep time: ______ **Cook time:** ______ **Servings:** ______

Ingredients

Directions

Notes

Recipe:____

Prep time:________   Cook time:________   Servings:________

Ingredients

Directions

Notes

Recipe:_______________________________________

Prep time:_______   Cook time:_______   Servings:_______

Ingredients

Directions

Notes

Recipe:_______________________________________

Prep time:_______   Cook time:_______   Servings:_______

Ingredients

Directions

Notes

www.ingramcontent.com/pod-product-compliance
Lightning Source LLC
Chambersburg PA
CBHW041833110726
48006CB00020B/2615